Preparing for a
Student Teacher

Student Teaching: The Cooperating Teacher Series

This series is designed exclusively for cooperating teachers. We like to say, "These are the little instruction books that should have come with the student teacher!" The series acknowledges the cooperating teacher's important role in the student teaching experience and gives key guidance for effective supervision:

> Book 1: *Preparing for a Student Teacher*
> Book 2: *Coaching a Student Teacher*
> Book 3: *Evaluating a Student Teacher*

The series is available as a set and as individual books so readers can explore the cooperating teacher role in totality or use the book that meets their current need. Each book offers essential techniques and practical advice. The user-friendly format provides a quick resource for the busy cooperating teacher to use in guiding the student teacher through a successful student teaching experience.

Preparing for a Student Teacher

Marvin A. Henry
and Ann Weber

ROWMAN & LITTLEFIELD
Lanham • Boulder • New York • London

Published by Rowman & Littlefield
A wholly owned subsidiary of The Rowman & Littlefield Publishing Group, Inc.
4501 Forbes Boulevard, Suite 200, Lanham, Maryland 20706
www.rowman.com

Unit A, Whitacre Mews, 26-34 Stannary Street, London SE11 4AB

British Library Cataloguing in Publication Information Available

Library of Congress Cataloging-in-Publication Data
Henry, Marvin A.
  Preparing for a student teacher / Marvin A. Henry and Ann Weber.
    pages cm
  Includes bibliographical references.
  ISBN 978-1-4758-2353-0 (pbk. : alk. paper) — ISBN 978-1-4758-2354-7
(electronic) 1. Student teachers—Supervision of. I. Weber, Ann. II. Title.
  LB2157.A3H448 2015
  370.71'1—dc23

                                                                    2015030151

∞™ The paper used in this publication meets the minimum requirements of
American National Standard for Information Sciences—Permanence of Paper
for Printed Library Materials, ANSI/NISO Z39.48-1992.

Printed in the United States of America

Contents

Preface

Ask persons in any profession where they learned the most beneficial knowledge in their practice and they will almost universally state that it was in the field with an experienced practitioner. They often tag the experience as the most exciting one too. The same is definitely true of teachers. As a cooperating teacher for the student teaching phase, YOU are the *experienced practitioner* in whose hands a student teacher has been placed. It is truly an honor!

However, once the wave of excitement settles, you realize the immense responsibility for the development of your student teacher and consequently his or her future students and the teaching profession as a whole. Your role in student teaching requires more than housing a budding professional and allowing him or her to absorb the tricks of the trade. Guiding a student teacher to the beginning teacher level requires a set of supervisory skills. If you have had little to no training in supervision, you suddenly begin to wonder just how qualified you are for this crucial role of shaping a future teacher.

We have vowed to try to do something to calm those what-do-I-do-now? anxieties. Wouldn't it be fantastic if all student teachers came with a little instruction book? Our hope is that you have found your way to this one, which promises to smoothly guide you through your role as cooperating teacher. Little doubt will be left about the supervisory skills that you need to create an exceptional student teaching environment.

We started by recognizing that busy teachers do not have time for laborious volumes of print to tell them what to do. Instead, we have digested the research and practice from the field and provide it in a set of brief workable volumes. This is the first of a series of three little instructional books using excerpts from our full text, *Supervising Student Teachers the Professional Way*, 7th edition.

Inside this book, you will find that research and experience are combined and illustrated with handy checklists and bulleted points. There are to-do lists where you can check a box when the task is completed and there are analytical worksheets to use. Each chapter also has a clipped "Note-to-Self" for readers to jot their ideas regarding the topic. The size and setup make each book a practical and useful companion. Of course, you are encouraged to explore additional concepts and practical advice by reading more deeply in the expanded version, but for now, this is a quick access to key points for your important role.

We believe that every cooperating teacher has different needs based upon where she or he falls in the timeline of the student teaching experience. Therefore, we have designed the series to focus on the following stages of the cooperating teacher role: the preparation, the coaching, and the evaluation. Cooperating teachers can use each book in the series as a guide for their current situation or use each to provide a heads-up for upcoming supervisory responsibilities.

Note our use of certain terminology in the book. We refer to the classroom instructor at the clinic school site as a *cooperating teacher* (CT). The undergraduate seeking a teaching degree is referred to as the *student teacher* (ST). The person who represents the university or college in a supervisory role is referred to as the *college supervisor* (CS). The use of pronouns that refer to men and women in these roles has been met by using "he" and "she" interchangeably.

We hope you enjoy the cooperating teacher journey as much as we have enjoyed preparing the map for you!

Ann Weber and Marvin Henry

Acknowledgments

Thank you to those heralded and unheralded cooperating teachers who supervise our future.

Thank you to the countless classroom teachers, college supervisors, field directors, teacher educators, student teachers, and professional friends who have helped us to pave the way for professional supervision of student teachers.

Thank you to Wayne Beasley and Ken Brighton for their contribution to early editions of *Supervising Student Teachers the Professional Way*.

Thank you to Roman & Littlefield's Tom Koerner, editor, and Carlie Wall, associate editor, for their attention to us and our works and then activating their publishing expertise to make things happen.

Thank you to Ruth and Charlie for encouragement and for sharing the Beef House dinner rolls.

Note to Self:

✓ CT uses supervisory skills.
✓ A plan for ST responsibilities is essential.
✓ The class & classroom need to be ready.
✓ ST requires acclimation to school & community.
✓

✓

Chapter 1

How Do I Get Ready?

In the few short months of student teaching, a college student completes the final required experience necessary to become a certified teacher. This is the last opportunity to develop the skills and attitudes that will inaugurate a teaching career. This transformation occurs under your watchful eye. You have consented to assume one of the most responsible, influential, and exciting roles in teacher education.

It can be a stimulating experience to have a student teacher in the classroom. Ganser and Wham (1998) report that cooperating teachers often felt personal satisfaction by giving professional guidance, providing an arena for beginning teachers to try their wings, being a role model, and contributing to the teaching profession. Gibbs and Montoya (1994) find that cooperating teachers believe that student teachers impact the professional development of cooperating teachers plus provide benefits for the classroom students. In spite of the increased responsibility involved, the experience of student teaching is a winning proposition for all parties.

A classroom is changed when a student teacher arrives. You will be working jointly and sharing responsibility with a person who is learning to teach. You will eventually surrender teaching and autonomy to this neophyte and assume the role of mentor and counselor. This change of roles places you in a new, exciting, and challenging position.

As a cooperating teacher, there are benefits. Moore (1995) identifies four areas of professional growth for those who mentor student teachers:

- Cooperating teachers can gain new ideas for innovation in the classroom.
- The student teacher helps create time to apply, analyze, and reflect on new experiences.
- The presence of the student teacher causes the cooperating teacher to plan more effectively, teach, and evaluate that teaching with a more discerning eye.
- A reflective perspective on classroom relationships develops between the cooperating teacher, the student teacher, and the students.

Additionally, Trenfield (1970) summarizes eight specific ways in which a student teacher's presence may improve classroom instruction. The possibilities seem to be as apparent today as when they were first written.

- The presence of a student teacher frequently is stimulating to both pupils and teacher.
- The presence of a student teacher requires the cooperating teacher to examine his own objectives and teaching strategies.
- The student teacher is sometimes a valuable source of ideas about instructional techniques and materials.
- Until the student teacher assumes all responsibility for instruction, there are two teachers in the classroom, enabling them to work as a team to plan and conduct activities.
- While the student teacher conducts class, the cooperating teacher is able to observe students from a different perspective, perhaps gaining valuable insight into their interests and learning.
- While the student teacher conducts classes, the cooperating teacher may work with individuals and small groups who need more special attention than normally can be given.

- As the student teacher assumes more responsibility, the cooperating teacher is freed to consult administrators and colleagues, to accumulate instructional materials, and to plan instruction for the future.
- Occasionally a pupil will relate much better to one adult than to another. The presence of a student teacher gives this pupil an additional opportunity to form a meaningful relationship with an adult.

UNDERSTANDING COOPERATING
TEACHER ROLE AND TRAITS

Those who are privileged to work with student teachers have both a great opportunity and an enormous responsibility in pointing the way for future educators. Costa and Garmston (1987) suggest that there are three major contributions that cooperating teachers and other educators can make to student teachers.

The first is *modeling*. Cooperating teachers model classroom practices, use of time and resources, instructional strategies, provisions for a safe and healthy learning environment, engagement of students, and use of assessments. They also model images of professional behavior in the classroom, on the playground, during faculty meetings, at conferences, and with parents.

The second contribution is *passing along tools of the trade*. Much has been learned about how certain teacher behaviors and choices impact student learning. Judgments must be made about the amount of instructional time allocated to various needs, such as how to give directions, elicit attention, handle distracting behavior, and manage classroom skills.

A third contribution is the *intellectual process of teaching*. This is the distinction between "know how" and "know why" that separates the professional educator from the novice teacher. This means cooperating teachers work with student teachers in guiding their thinking about planning, teaching, analyzing, and evaluating, and applying what they have learned to future actions.

As a cooperating teacher, you must be an exemplary classroom teacher as well as an effective supervisor and be willing to devote many hours to help a student evolve into a teacher. Barnes and Edwards (1984) report that cooperating teachers in the more effective experiences:

- Were more proactive than reactive.
- Were more specific in their communication.
- Modeled the behaviors, teaching techniques, and attitudes they recommended to the student teachers.
- Exhibited greater consistency between their behaviors and their verbal expressions.

- Were more adaptable and flexible.
- Provided rationales for their actions and suggestions.
- Practiced self-reflection as an active learner.
- Employed positive, problem-solving approaches.

PREPPING FOR THE EXPERIENCE

It is essential to prepare for the arrival of a student teacher. Adequate preparation reduces anxiety for both the cooperating teacher and the student teacher. Many arrangements are necessary before a student teacher arrives. The initial ones require some investigation. The most obvious search points include:

☐ Reading and understanding the college student teaching handbook.

☐ Becoming aware of any campus requirements for the student teacher.

☐ Becoming aware of the legal status of student teachers in the school district and state.

☐ Making necessary arrangements for the student teacher's presence.

   An adult-size desk or table and chair
   Name plate to door entry and desk
   Necessary office supplies
   Files of essential information
   Manuals and resources
   Computer access

☐ Informing appropriate administration, faculty, and staff of the decision to host a student teacher and the impact on their work environment.

MAPPING THE FRAMEWORK OF RESPONSIBILITY

A key element in building a strong student teaching experience is designing a reasonable plan for the assumption of responsibilities by the student teacher. The value of preplanning for the student teaching experience should not be underestimated. While this task may take considerable time, mapping the experience provides a clear and purposeful guide for you and the student teacher.

No matter how competent and confident, student teachers need a slow, gradual building of responsibilities. After you consider all the nonteaching and instructional responsibilities of the classroom, systematically plan what the student teacher will assume each week of the experience. Each week, a typical plan might add one or two nonteaching duties and one instructional duty. A progressive guide to keep in mind when mapping each new responsibility for the student teacher follows:

1. *Observe and listen.* Prior to taking on any responsibility, the plan should include time to explain and demonstrate the procedure and the reason behind the procedure.
2. *Collaborate.* Plan one or two opportunities for you and your student teacher to work together on the newest nonteaching or teaching task. This includes the planning and implementation. The time spent as a team will provide the student teacher with valuable insights and a safety net. Collaborate on one new responsibility at a time before allowing the student teacher independence. In time you will repeat the procedure for the next new responsibility.
3. *Designate gradually.* The student teaching experience emphasizes quality rather than quantity. The gradual assumption of responsibility allows the student teacher to master each skill and each group of pupils with competency and confidence before the next task is added. Many set the goal for half of the responsibilities to be assumed by midpoint of the experience.
4. *Delegate all.* After the midpoint, the remaining responsibilities can be assumed at a quicker pace. Each college may require a different number of weeks for full responsibilities. Three to four weeks is a reasonable amount of time for the student teacher to demonstrate his teacher abilities.
5. *Reduce.* Once the full-time experience concludes, there is an ending transition period. The student teacher and cooperating teacher co-plan and co-teach one or two lessons for each class period before gradually letting the cooperating teacher regain each of the individual teaching responsibilities. Nonteaching responsibilities are also returned gradually.

This progression is flexible. The individuality of a student teacher is a variable that can determine the pace and the order of responsibilities. Students, curriculum, and administration may also make it necessary for the plan to be altered as the student teaching experience progresses.

Keeping the above progression in mind, the following excerpts of a total plan are offered as a sample of how a framework might be constructed for the typical student teacher placed in an elementary setting to *gradually* assume and return responsibilities for all the nonteaching and teaching experiences.

Responsibility Plan for Student Teacher

Week	Non-Teaching	Teaching
1	Take attendance Discuss procedure for grading Attend meetings Observe grade above and below	Circulate to assist students Learn names of students Distribute materials Record assignments on front board and online
2	Grade Math homework Design bulletin board Add section to Parent Newsletter Observe specialty classes	Co-plan & co-teach Math lessons
3	Discuss/demo on Monday: Collect for field trip Pet and plant care Grade reading homework Walk students to specials	Independently plan and teach Math Prepare math work and discuss with aide and tutors R-F Co-plan and co-teach one small Reading group
4	After-recess Chapter Book Plan new seating arrangement	Teach Math, one Reading group R-F Co-plan and co-teach second reading group
⋮		
11-13	Full responsibility	Full responsibility
⋮		
14	Return to CT: attendance, bulletin boards, newsletter, math and reading homework grading Observe three teachers in building.	Return to CT: Math, Reading, Art, Spelling,
15	Observe another district school Mock Interview	Return to CT: Science Assist with seatwork Monitor Learning Centers and Computers Practice "subbing" for two lessons using CT's sub plans

Co-teaching is gaining popularity as a format for student teaching. The assumption of independent duties can also be a gradual process by having the student teacher transition from a brief period as observer to teaching as planned by the cooperating teacher, to collaborative planning and teaching, and finally to leading the instructional planning.

Gone are the days when the student teacher walked into the classroom as the cooperating teacher walked out. Student teachers learn by watching, interacting, and reflecting with cooperating teachers as well as by their own application and exploration. However, having a solid plan to start the experience adds comfort and purpose for both the cooperating teacher and student teacher.

LEARNING ABOUT A STUDENT TEACHER

You will want to know something about the incoming student teacher in order to plan appropriate initial activities. Acquaintances can best be made through face-to-face contact but phone conversations and written communication are options. Once contact has been made, appropriate adjustments to the Responsibility Plan can be made. The following list is a helpful start in securing information about your new student teacher:

Student Teacher Information

☐ Educational Background

College courses completed in major and minor areas
Prior clinical experiences
Experiences with children or youth
Technology skill level
Additional language competencies
Special honors or awards
Extracurricular involvement

☐ General Experiences

Employment
Community service
Leadership responsibilities
Travel
Recreational interests
Hobbies

☐ Educational Philosophy

☐ Professional Goals

☐ Expectations for Student Teaching

☐ Contact Information

ACCLIMATING THE STUDENT TEACHER

The student teacher journeys through a series of concerns prior to and during student teaching. Many initial concerns center around the school and community settings. A cooperating teacher who has lived in the community and taught in its school system for some time may fail to realize that the setting may be vastly different from the one the student teacher has experienced.

Acquainting your student teacher with your school and community setting prior to the beginning of the experience can easily be accomplished through a pre-student teaching visit along with written and

Acclimation Information

- **General School Information**
  - Type of population served
  - Philosophy, goals, and mission statement
  - School report card
  - School improvement plan
  - School schedule
  - Layout of the facilities
  - School phone, address
  - School website
  - Handbooks
  - Administration, faculty and support staff
  - School Board
  - Guest check-in procedure
- **Classroom Information**
  - Teaching manuals
  - Instructional resources
  - Technology resources and access
  - Reporting procedures
  - Grading policies
  - Student background
  - Classroom website address
  - Classroom layout
  - Seating chart
  - First Aid
- **School Policies Relating to the Faculty**
  - Arrival and departure times
  - Assigned responsibilities
  - Appropriate dress
  - Right of privacy information
  - Distribution of medication
  - Technology usage
  - Faculty identification
  - Lunch purchases
- **School Policies Relating to Students**
  - Dress
  - Discipline
  - Student activities
  - Electronic devices
  - Grades as related to extracurricular activities
  - Zero tolerance
- **Forms and Reports**
  - Grade forms
  - Attendance reports
  - Accident reports
  - Field trip request
  - Special services request
  - Detention notice
  - Equipment request
- **General Community Information**
  - Population
  - Diversity
  - Social economic structure
  - Business district
  - Major employers
  - City map
  - City governance
  - City website address
  - Historical facts

- **Emergency Procedures**
  - Fires
  - Weather-related incidents
  - Natural disaster drills
  - Violence prevention and reporting
  - Lock down procedure
  - Conflict resolution
- **Specific Information about Students**
  - Pupil records
  - Personality characteristics
  - Special needs and accommodations
  - Class roster
  - Seating chart
- **Schedule of Classes**
  - Teacher weekly schedule
  - Student weekly schedule
- **School Directory**
- **School Calendar**
- **Location of Key Areas**
  - Grade levels or departments
  - Office suite
  - Work room
  - Cafeteria
  - Teacher's lounge
  - Library
  - Media center
  - Computer center
  - Technology support office
  - Guidance office
  - Health services
  - Faculty parking lots
- **Service Facilities**
  - Procedure for reproducing materials
  - Media resources
  - Technology for instructors
  - Technology for students
  - Classroom supplies
  - Teacher equipment
- **Extracurricular Programs**
  - List of programs
  - Types of duties
  - Schedule of events
  - Expectations
- **Responsibility Plan for Student Teacher**

- **Neighborhood Surrounding the School**
- **Living Accommodations**
- **Restaurants**
- **Community Transportation**
- **Recreational Facilities**
- **Local Newspaper**
- **Local Radio Station**
- **Local Community Events**
- **Places of Interest**

electronic resources. Some cooperating teachers construct a binder or flash drive of information which serves as a long-term resource for the student teacher.

Many pieces of information which are essential can be found via student and faculty handbooks, school and community newspapers, class and faculty rosters, school and community Web sites, maps, plus tours of the school and community. The preceding checklist serves as a guide to the acclimation of the student teacher.

PREPARING THE CLASS

A teacher begins to establish a student teacher's status with the class before the arrival date. The pupils ought to know that a student teacher is coming and anticipate this event with some enthusiasm. If pupils are provided with clear and accurate information about the purposes and processes of the student teaching experience, they can become partners in preparing future teachers. Typical preparation activities include:

- Creating anticipation that the student teacher will bring interesting, worthwhile learning experiences to the classroom.
- Describing the purposes of student teaching.
- Informing students of the proper respect and trust to be given to this adult who will assume teacher status in their classroom.
- Explaining how the members of the class can help the student teacher.
- Assigning specific students to acclimate the student teacher by providing information on student organizations, activities, and typical student school schedule.
- Encouraging the student teacher to visit the assigned school at least once prior to the start of the student teaching experience or to send a short note of introduction.

The potential for a successful student teaching experience starts before the student teaching time begins. Your thoughtful and careful attention to the cooperating teacher role and the preparation for the student teacher's arrival will have a lasting impact on the experience.

```
┌──────────────────────────────────────────────────┐
│                                           ╭─╮     │
│   **Note to Self:**                       │ │     │
│                                           │ │     │
│   ✓  Change is ahead & that is okay.      │ │     │
│   ✓  Introductions need to be planned.    │ │     │
│   ✓  Meaningful activities are a must.    ╰─╯     │
│   ✓  Roles & responsibilities lead to teaching.  │
│   ✓                                              │
│                                                  │
│   ✓                                              │
│                                                  │
└──────────────────────────────────────────────────┘
```

Chapter 2

How Do I Get the Student Teacher Started?

Your student teacher may have participated in a number of exploratory field experiences, but student teaching is the long-anticipated learning sequence closest to reality. The first days are critical to the systematic development of your student teacher so he will have the skill and confidence necessary to independently direct a classroom.

Kagan (1992) analyzed over forty studies relating to teacher development and concludes that preservice and beginning teachers' growth consists of at least five components. Her research will remind you of the professional growth ahead for your student teacher.

- A developing awareness of initial and changing knowledge and beliefs about pupils and classrooms.
- A reconstruction of idealized and inaccurate images of students and a reconstruction of early images of self as teacher.
- A shift in attention to students and instruction upon resolution of one's own professional identity.
- Acquiring and becoming comfortable with standard classroom procedures.
- Growth in problem-solving skills.

Your student teacher may be aware that changes are going to occur but may not know what will take place. A cooperating teacher understands the pattern of growth that is anticipated and is prepared to help the new student teacher as the experience progresses.

CHANGES IN THE CLASSROOM

The arrival of your student teacher brings about a change in your classroom environment that is sensed by both you and your students. The change in environment encompasses the totality of the classroom so be prepared to modify the way things are done. Change can be a positive element in your classroom, and *different* should not automatically be construed as *deficient*.

A pre-student teaching visit and communication about expectations provide some degree of preparedness for the impending change, but only the physical presence of a student teacher provides the full impact of this different educational climate. The well-prepared student teacher, appropriately involved in the classroom and working in concert with you, will be an asset rather than a liability to student learning.

You begin to include the student teacher in the classroom by sharing your space, responsibilities, and pupils. You will also need to:

- ☐ Update the student teacher about the classroom routines and management techniques.
- ☐ Apprise the student teacher of the class work that is currently under way.
- ☐ Involve the student teacher in meaningful activities.
- ☐ Reorient the student teacher to the school.
- ☐ Schedule observations for the student teacher in other classrooms.

Cotton (1981) wisely advises what and what not to do when a student teacher arrives. Some of the suggestions for cooperating teachers are:

- Tell the student teacher what you are doing and why.
- Listen to your student teacher and allow the student teacher to ask questions of you.
- Do not undercut the value of a teacher preparation program. It is not helpful to criticize the program that prepared the student to teach.
- Do not compare one student teacher with another.

INTRODUCTION TO THE CLASS

The first few days are periods of adjustment and learning for everyone in the classroom. You may be as nervous as the student teacher wondering how the experience will evolve. Do not forget that your pupils also wonder about the new situation. What is the student teacher like? What changes will there be? What does the cooperating teacher think of the student teacher? Some pupils will vie for the attention of the student teacher and may even act differently. A new mood permeates your classroom.

Your student teacher should not simply enter the classroom and begin to participate. A proper introduction is necessary. The introduction of a student teacher does more than present a name to a group of pupils. It is a process of communicating feelings and ascribing status. This may be the most obvious clue for the pupils in perceiving your attitude toward this beginner.

The introduction defines the roles of the student teacher, the cooperating teacher, and the students. Since the introduction may affect relationships during the entire student teaching sequence, select your words carefully. These considerations are worthy of emphasis in designing an effective introduction:

- ☐ Welcome the student teacher. Show sincerity at having this person as part of the class. Use personal expressions to show a feeling of acceptance.

- ☐ Recognize the competency of your student teacher. Specify major areas of study and describe any unique experiences, special skills, or achievements that he has.

- ☐ Introduce the student as a *teacher*. This will assign status and authority.

- ☐ Indicate confidence in your student teacher. Project the feeling that the classroom will be improved because of his presence. Indicate some projects or learning activities that are possible now with the extra teacher present.

- ☐ Give your student teacher an opportunity to briefly speak to the class. Let him know this ahead of time so he is prepared.

- ☐ In a preplanned way, pupils may briefly present a written or verbal welcome greeting.

INTRODUCTION TO THE FACULTY

Interaction with the faculty is as much a growth experience as many other activities during student teaching because relationships with other teachers help formulate professional behavior. Your student teacher's previous contacts with teachers have been mostly as pupils; now they are associates.

There is much to be learned about teaching through association with colleagues. The encouragement and assistance of teachers in the school can be very helpful to a student teacher. Teachers within the school can provide instructional ideas and share insights for the same grade level or content areas. Some teachers play a direct part in learning by allowing student teachers to observe them teach.

Although you are the supervising teacher, the student teacher will be reassured throughout the school day when recognized by other colleagues. The introduction can be made in a manner that provides recognition and acceptance of the student teacher. The following procedures may be of value in acquainting your student teacher with the teaching staff:

- ☐ Make it known that a student teacher is coming to work with you. An official school announcement, newspaper, or faculty e-mail can list the name and arrival date of your student teacher.
- ☐ Introduce the student teacher at faculty meetings and at informed settings such as the teacher's lounge, workroom, or hallway.
- ☐ Make comments that will help your student teacher know and remember others, such as indicating a faculty member's responsibilities and classroom location.
- ☐ Arrange for the student teacher to eat lunch with you and a small group of colleagues.
- ☐ Arrange times to be spent with other teachers without your presence.

INITIAL DAYS

The student teacher's initiation into the classroom is critical because it sets the stage for her future role as an instructor. The student teacher will not usually be leading instruction during these beginning days because there is much to learn before taking that responsibility. This does not mean that you will have your student teacher sit and observe for days because that will result in boredom and anxiety.

Starting with the first day of student teaching, your student teacher can participate in noninstructional activities that make a contribution to the class. There are many worthwhile teaching activities that can be performed without extensive preparation or orientation. Some of the more common early activities which you can plan for your student teacher include:

- Checking attendance
- Grading assignments
- Operating equipment
- Distributing and collecting papers and materials
- Assisting with seatwork
- Assisting with laboratory project work
- Helping pupils with computer activity
- Working with individuals or small groups
- Assisting with make-up work
- Assisting with supervision of study periods
- Assisting with supervision of recess periods
- Designing PowerPoints to be used by the cooperating teacher
- Loading computer programs
- Searching for helpful instructional Web sites
- Gathering resources and materials
- Reading literature aloud
- Assisting the teacher with demonstrations
- Planning and creating a display, learning center, or bulletin board
- Listing assignments on the board and online classroom site

A student teacher will find it advantageous to be seated at a place in the room where eye contact can be made with all learners. This helps to establish the feeling that a teacher, rather than a visitor, is in the room. It increases awareness of classroom dynamics and will facilitate learning the names of the pupils. With proper positioning, you are also more likely to seek the assistance of a nearby student teacher in minor but necessary tasks.

INCREASED RESPONSIBILITY

As the cooperating teacher, you can assign tasks that build confidence in the student teacher. It is a bonus for your student teacher when he is asked to work with learners who need assistance, perform tasks that demand special skills, or be used as a resource person. Walker and Archer (1999) identify specific "Roles and Goals" that student teachers can assume early in their experience:

- *Clarifier*—restate ideas or directions to students who have difficulty staying focused.
- *Progress Coach*—help students master content by giving feedback concerning individual progress during lessons.

- *Individual Motivator*—encourage students to maintain a positive attitude and to participate in class activity.
- *Taskmaster*—continually monitor and keep students on task and use positive statements to refocus student behavior.
- *Individual Facilitator*—direct and guide an individual student throughout an entire activity.
- *Small-Group Monitor*—stay within close proximity of a group, observing and recording behavior that can be given as feedback to the lead teacher.
- *Small-Group Facilitator*—direct and guide group activities such as providing the group with materials, equalizing participation, clarifying directions, reteaching skills, or providing feedback.
- *Large-Group Facilitator*—act as facilitator for one group when class is divided into two groups following a lesson.

The roles and tasks of the classroom teacher which have been mentioned above are established habits for you, but they are new for the student teacher. Rather than assume the student teacher understands and knows the details of any new responsibility, time should be taken to fully acquaint him with the duty. Use think-aloud and demonstration strategies before your student teacher takes on the new role or task.

INITIAL INSTRUCTION

This chapter provides ways of moving student teachers gradually toward major instructional responsibilities. Success in the described tasks and roles during the initial weeks will pave the way for the more demanding and more exciting teaching activities in the weeks ahead.

When your student teacher does finally begin assuming an instructional responsibility, which is common during the second week, recall the value of the gradual assumption of teaching responsibilities. Confidence and competencies can be achieved before the student teacher earns instructional independence by using these stages:

1. Observation
2. Think Aloud
3. Co-planning
4. Co-teaching
5. Cooperating teacher as assistant
6. Independence

A quick survey of the student teacher's activities gives an appraisal of progress toward initial adjustment to this new life as a teacher. If the right proportion of responsibilities has been assigned, within the first two weeks your student teacher should:

- ☐ Know the names of pupils.
- ☐ Have some professional knowledge about the pupils.
- ☐ Be independent in moving about the school.
- ☐ Have met a number of other teachers and feel comfortable with them.
- ☐ Have observed teachers, including those in other grade levels or subjects.
- ☐ Contribute valuable ideas during joint planning sessions.
- ☐ Be able to make one to two initial plans without the cooperating teacher's direct supervision.
- ☐ Have taken an opportunity for teaching an entire class.
- ☐ Be reflective about his work.

It is not unusual for beginning student teachers to report that they are fatigued at the end of the day. The pressure of adjusting to the new and demanding role of a teacher consumes more energy than one might assume. This situation will likely rectify itself in a few days but it might be well at this time to remind your student teacher that teaching can be emotionally draining and physically exhausting. The student teacher should not be overprotected, though, since being tired is a normal part of a teacher's life.

Note to Self:

✓ Differences can be assets.

✓ ST expects, desires, & needs feedback.

✓ CT sets climate for guidance & emotional support.

✓ ST grows in professional skills, relationships, & identity.

✓

✓

Chapter 3

How Do I Build a Working Relationship with a Student Teacher?

Student teachers have strong needs for professional guidance as well as emotional support so you, as cooperating teacher, must establish a supportive emotional and professional climate. A typical period of adjustment in the relationship is always expected, yet there are specific cooperating teacher traits which you can activate to build a positive and productive relationship with your student teacher.

- Being available.
- Spelling out expectations early.
- Establishing and maintaining communication.
- Giving the student teacher some options and choices.
- Giving the student teacher the opportunity to develop her own style.
- Accepting the student teacher as a colleague.
- Including the student teacher in more than the immediate environment of the classroom.
- Seeking and using the student teacher's ideas whenever possible.
- Demonstrating confidence and trust in the student teacher.
- Referring to *our* students and *our* classroom.

Looper (1999) asked student teachers to list qualities of cooperating teachers that they valued. The following list prompts cooperating teachers of ways to build the relationship.

- Provide encouragement.
- Avoid putting student teachers in difficult situations.
- Provide honest and timely feedback.
- Communicate often and freely.
- Share insights about the students.
- Discuss successful teaching techniques.
- Allow them to experience the excitement of learning, as well as mundane tasks.
- Let student teachers "try their wings."
- Set regular times to conference with student teachers.
- Give suggestions about planning.
- Be flexible.
- Be a receptive listener to ideas and concerns.
- Instruct the student teacher about classroom management.
- Show how to organize time and space for effective instruction.
- Share tips for success.
- Be a positive role model.

In addition to the above lists, the following self-examination can be used throughout the student teaching experience to analyze the cooperating teacher's supportive nature.

Relationship-Building Traits of Cooperating Teachers

1. I accept my student teacher as a professional colleague as evidenced by:

    ☐ Showing respect for my student teacher's decisions.

    ☐ Allowing my student teacher to assume responsibility.

    ☐ Listening to my student teacher's ideas and concerns.

☐ Using relevant ideas submitted by my student teacher.

☐ Permitting my student teacher to assume the same privileges that I have.

2. I accept the usual mistakes of my student teacher as evidenced by:

☐ Refraining from overreacting to mistakes.

☐ Allowing my student teacher to continue with responsibilities.

☐ Stating that mistakes are normal and most are not irreversible.

3. I refrain from prescriptive directions as evidenced by:

☐ Discussing options with my student teacher before a decision is made.

☐ Allowing freedom of choice on the part of my student teacher.

☐ Engaging in professional dialog to set goals for my student teacher.

4. I conduct professional discussions with my student teacher as evidenced by discussions about:

☐ Learning problems of students.

☐ Teaching methodologies, their applications, and the results.

☐ Using a variety of assessments.

☐ Monitoring student behavior.

☐ Exhibiting a professional image.

5. I allow my student teacher to observe and discuss my instructional activities and teacher effectiveness as evidenced by:

☐ Requesting an analysis of my lessons.

☐ Asking for suggestions for alternative procedures.

6. I diagnose learners' interests and needs, develop learning strategies, and share these procedures with my student teacher as evidenced by:

☐ Discussing diagnostic procedures.

☐ Explaining why conclusions were reached.

☐ Encouraging my student teacher to be involved in the development of Individual Education Plans (IEPs) and Universal Designed Instruction (UDI).

☐ Explaining why certain teaching techniques will be used as a result of the diagnosis and analysis.

CONSTRUCTIVE CLIMATE

Every cooperating teacher offers feedback and advice to the student teacher. Providing the positive aspects is often easier than pointing out the negative aspects, but both are very necessary. Both are deemed a positive piece in the developmental process and expected in the professional relationship.

Grossman and Keller (1994) state that the ability to give meaningful feedback to student teachers is of utmost importance. The research of Seiferth and Samuel (1984) reveals that student teachers want and need constant, ongoing feedback given in a tactful, polite way. The findings suggest that cooperating teachers create pitfalls if they fail to offer critiques.

There is no single way to approach feedback constructively. A strategy that produces high success while avoiding a critical, dominant, or insincere tone is to connect your feedback to student outcome and to the goal of professional growth for the student teacher. In the case of a weakness, improvements for the sake of the learners and for increased professional skills are solid and heartfelt reasons for student teachers to change. This works much better than comments which appear to criticize. The strategy will also work as praise when cooperating teachers acknowledge successful student teacher decisions.

To build a climate where feedback is nonthreatening and considered helpful, consider what Babkie (1998) identifies as ways to maintain a trusting and low-stress environment:

- Try to eliminate problems before they start.
- Provide specific feedback.
- Have a regular and frequent meeting time.
- Allow the student teacher to make mistakes.
- Support, encourage, and reward a student teacher's progress.
- Accept differences in the student teacher's approach.
- Evaluate yourself as well as the student teacher.

TRANSITION OF THE STUDENT TEACHER

The student teacher enters student teaching often unaware of the personal adjustments that are necessary for a teacher. As the cooperating teacher provides guidance, he also provides perspective. The following topics are ones you may need to address as your student teacher transitions into the teacher role. Some may be sensitive topics, but whom better than the cooperating teacher (with the possible aid of the college supervisor) to promptly and compassionately bring these to the attention of the future teacher. The following clearly have an impact at the student teaching level and also in future professional relationships.

Collaboration

Teachers often work in a collaborative fashion by interacting with other teachers, administrators, parents, and aides. Student teachers have a range of collaborative ability. Therefore, it is wise for the student teacher and cooperating teacher to examine interpersonal qualities that increase the chance for successful collaboration.

Share the following checklist with your student teacher for analysis and feedback concerning attributes that are critical to collaborative success. The awareness and strengthening of these by the student teacher minimize potential problems in the school setting.

Student Teacher Interpersonal Checklist

		3-Excellent 2-Satisfactory 1-Unacceptable
ATTRIBUTE	**COMMENTS**	**RATING**
Attendance		
Punctuality		
Oral Expression		
Written Expression		
Interactions with Others		
Reliability & Dependability		
Initiative		
Collegiality		
Professionalism		
Response to Feedback		
Cooperation		
Decision Making		

Self-Concept

Student teaching can be anxiety producing when feelings of self-adequacy and security are threatened. Self-concept is undoubtedly affected by the importance that is placed on success in student teaching. It is complicated by the fact that student teaching is a new experience. This newness can initiate an emotional cycle that runs from elation to dejection. This innovation cycle seems to be typical of any new experience and involves different reactions at various stages. This was noted by Sharpe (1970) and has been adjusted to a typical ten-week experience in the following figure.

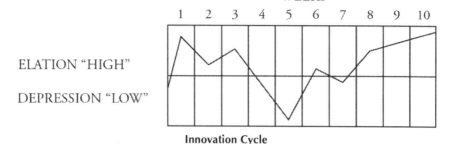

Innovation Cycle

Your student teacher most likely enters the experience with some feelings of insecurity and fear. These initial concerns lessen as he is welcomed by the staff and meets the students so the first peak of enthusiasm may be reached after a few days. Typically, a rather sharp emotional decline will occur around the fourth or fifth week. This may be caused by such factors as an altercation with a pupil, poor performance on students' tests, or increased responsibilities. Finally, there will be a gradual building of confidence and satisfaction.

The cooperating teacher is in a position to temper the student teacher's emotions if aware of this normal phenomenon. You can anticipate and proactively assist with self-concept feelings. One example of this is by sharing in your student teacher's feeling of success by verbalizing her decisions which led to the positive outcome you witnessed. An example of what to do when you recognize that your student teacher is feeling low is to share a hopeful story about a challenge you overcame during your own student teaching days. Whether written or verbal, the extra attention and support that you give to your student during the peaks and valleys are helpful.

Teacher Identity

Student teachers of all ages, abilities, and maturity levels typically have some difficulty finding their identities during student teaching. She may appear at the school looking like a teacher, but this appearance does not guarantee maturity. The pupils call her a teacher; the college personnel regard her as a student; and the cooperating teacher considers her to be a teacher one moment and a student the next.

Many situations can trigger identity issues. Meeting students in the community, attending afterschool events, and parent-teacher conferences are new to her role. A student teacher may experience difficulty distinguishing between "a friendly teacher" and "a friend." There is the possibility that a student teacher could become the target of a romantic gesture from a pupil. A student teacher may also seem more comfortable in the company of pupils because interactions with adults in the school setting can initially seem intimidating or awkward.

As the student teacher becomes more visibly active in her role, the teacher identity problem lessens; however, the student teacher needs to be keenly attentive to presenting a professional image throughout the experience. Your help is needed to present the novice with opportunities, situations, and well-timed discussions that help her settle quickly and appropriately into her professional role and behavior.

Professional Rapport with Pupils

Developing appropriate rapport with pupils will take time for the student teacher. You can help the student teacher develop appropriate pupil-teacher relationships but abstract discussions are not always the best method. The following items can assist you in advancing your student teacher's rapport with his pupils.

- ☐ Have your student teacher assume responsibility gradually.
- ☐ Explain why you have established certain procedures and rules.
- ☐ Identify unusual behavioral patterns of pupils and counsel with your student teacher before unfortunate moves are made.
- ☐ Caution your student teacher not to make threats or disciplinary sanctions that cannot be carried out.
- ☐ Point out that pupils want their teacher to act like an adult.
- ☐ Stress that genuine respect from a class is achieved from such factors as enthusiasm, respect, listening, and interesting class sessions.
- ☐ Explain that respect takes time to earn but can be destroyed in an instant.
- ☐ Help your student teacher understand pupils and their lifestyles.
- ☐ Suggest readings about positive pupil-teacher relationships.
- ☐ Remind your student teacher that classroom management involves more than discipline.
- ☐ Suggest your student teacher implement established procedures before introducing new ones.
- ☐ Discuss the impact of appearance, words, and actions.

It is sometimes difficult to convince student teachers that their words and actions affect pupil behavior. If this is the problem, the following questions may be useful to a student teacher in analyzing her rapport with pupils. You can assist the student teacher by identifying supporting examples and adding ways to increase projection of each quality.

Analysis for Student Teacher–Pupil Rapport

1. Do I show enthusiasm so that my students are aware of the interest that I have in specific subjects and teaching in general?
2. Am I courteous to pupils and show them respect and, in turn, command respect from them?
3. Do I insist that my students treat others with courtesy and respect?
4. Do I recognize good work as much as or more than I criticize poor student accomplishment?
5. Do I make assignments that are clear and justify those assignments in terms of their value to students?
6. Do I make an effort to provide for individual differences?
7. Do I use a variety of teaching procedures to avoid monotony and to appeal to student interests and learning styles?
8. Do I attempt to make every student in my classes feel some personal responsibility for the effectiveness of my class?
9. Do my students believe that my goal is to help them learn?
10. Do I believe that my main purpose in teaching is to help students and be an advocate for them?
11. Do I present a teacher image through words, dress, and actions?

Working with a student teacher requires that you expect personal differences to exist. Any differences can be accepted as long as effective teaching and learning are not jeopardized. When you recognize differences and realize that one style is not superior to another, you can determine whether the current situation requires a professional discussion with your student teacher or if you need to accept her preference as a professional option.

The two following categories often surface as points of concern. A self-assessment by the cooperating teacher may uncover a preference rather than a problem. When the matter is more than preference, the issue can be tempered by focusing on the professional aspect of the matter during a discussion with your student teacher.

PERSONALITY DIFFERENCES

The student teacher's personality may be similar to or quite different than yours. The aim is to make them complementary rather than competitive or adversarial. When personalities are recognized, adjustments to communication in the relationship can be made because the workable relationship depends on recognizing how best to approach and draw strengths from each other.

Myers and Myers (1980) provide a psychological type format that Shaw-Baker (1995) uses to identify four personality aspects that may surface when student teachers and cooperating teachers communicate. Recognizing differences or similarities helps in appreciating alternative perspectives and choosing an effective approach for communication.

- *Extroversion and introversion.* Extroverts are energized by all the events and their preference is to talk things out. Introverts are stimulated by their inner thoughts and need periods of privacy to reflect upon their experiences.
- *Information gathering.* Some people want the facts and are not as concerned about the theory behind them. Other individuals prefer links between cause and effect and can put the symptoms of a problem into the bigger picture.
- *Making decisions.* One type of personality decides a plan of action based upon logic. Another prefers decisions which include personal, subjective values.
- *Lifestyle.* Some lifestyles are more orderly and planned while others prefer a more spontaneous and flexible style.

Identifying your student teacher's preferences allows you to better understand the student teacher's natural thought process and choices and to know that their decisions are not intentionally meant to clash with yours. Professional partnerships do not require identical personalities; in fact, differences can be complementary.

GENERATIONAL DIFFERENCES

You may initially note generational differences in your student teacher's use of technology, dress, or verbiage. It is likely that your student teacher will note differences in you as well. The gap between the two of you can provide a positive dimension to the classroom. The student teacher brings current teaching strategies to the experience and you share strategies used throughout your tenure. Interacting with each other throughout the student teaching experience will broaden skills and perspectives of *both* of you.

Generational differences can have a negative impact if the student teacher does not recognize how words, actions, and appearance can negatively impact their image in the teacher role. Your guidance can help the student teacher to become aware that while acceptable in other circles, these same choices may be inappropriate within the school setting. Discussions need not criticize the student teacher's personal choices, but will have a greater influence when you emphasize the impact and impression the student teacher's image is having on the students and members of the school community.

INTENSE DIFFERENCES

Differences between the cooperating teacher and student teacher can add zest and balance to a classroom, provided that not all energy is put into emphasizing the dissimilarities and conflicts. There are instances when the differences are too extreme. Certain incompatibilities make it difficult for the student teaching experience to be successful. It may be better to terminate the current student teaching placement but not before some remedies are tried.

A sincere self-evaluation of the variables mentioned in this chapter can determine whether you add to or subtract from the relationship. A review of the discussions with and remediation attempts by the student teacher is also essential. Additionally, the college supervisor must be approached as a valued resource in determining if the working relationship has reached an unacceptable level.

A cooperating teacher can often avoid the escalation of a relationship problem, improve the outcome of tense situations, and ease difficult discussions when a positive working relationship has already been established. Here are constructive actions to implement:

- Recognize and accept the differences without trying to convince the other that you are right.
- View the variation in style as an asset rather than a liability.
- Attempt alternative communication with less emphasis on conflict.
- Plan autonomous activities so that both have independence but you can still observe performance.
- Arrange for your student teacher to have time with other teachers with whom she can feel comfortable.
- Verbalize new strategies and techniques learned from the student teacher.
- Recognize your student teacher's intentions even when success is not achieved.

Building a successful working relationship with your student teacher takes time. Being aware of what impacts the relationship and giving attention to the factors which you can control are essential supervisory steps toward that goal.

Chapter 4

How Do I Interact with the College Supervisor?

College supervisors assume a unique role among professional educators. They work in cooperating school settings but are not on the faculty. As a part of the college, they may work solely with student teachers or they may share dual responsibility for teaching college courses and supervising student teachers. They may also be former professors, teachers, school administrators, or possibly doctoral students. Regardless of their background, the college supervisor is a person who enhances the student teaching experience and completes the triad of key players in the student teaching experience.

Most would agree with the research of Zimpher (1980) that without the motivating presence of the college supervisor, student teaching would have a rather flat profile. She found that the supervisor fills roles that would have been otherwise overlooked. Giebelhaus (1995) concludes that frequent contact with the college supervisor and direct contact among all members of the triad also means less isolation and less anxiety.

ROLES AND RESPONSIBILITIES

As cooperating teacher, you are in contact with the college supervisor at the school setting and possibly via phone or Internet conversations. The college supervisor has a wide scope of professional responsibilities tied to his position yet cooperating teachers are often unaware of those. The following list describes the numerous roles that college supervisors may perform. Cooperating teachers who are aware of these overlapping roles will more likely come to accept, appreciate, and use the services of this unique individual.

- *Placement consultant.* The college supervisor makes contact with college and cooperating school personnel to implement appropriate placements for student teachers under his charge.
- *Orientation advisor.* He is responsible for making the student teacher and cooperating teacher aware of the student teaching requirements and responsibilities.
- *Instructor.* The teaching role of the college supervisor is manifested through individualized instruction for each student teacher. This involves simple ideas, complex analysis, ongoing feedback, and evaluation of students' program and state certification work.
- *Seminar director.* Many student teaching programs require the college supervisor to provide regular seminars on professional topics for groups of student teachers.
- *Counselor.* A college supervisor is called to be responsive to the personal and professional problems existing with or anticipated by a student teacher.
- *Liaison.* He interprets the college program to the cooperating school and explains the cooperating school's program to the appropriate personnel at the college.
- *Supervisor.* As a teacher educator, he helps to improve instruction and to maximize the growth and development of student teachers through lesson plan analysis, classroom observation, data collection, and conferences.
- *Consultant.* He serves the public school by informally or formally sharing a variety of topics. His knowledge and experience provide new ideas and information to public school personnel.

- *Evaluator*. He provides formative and summative assessments, decides whether college requirements have been met, and submits a final evaluation or grade.
- *Representative*. The college supervisor represents the college, its education program, and a member of the teaching profession.

EARLY INTERACTION

One of the initial responsibilities of the college supervisor is to acquaint the cooperating teacher with the expectations of the college's student teaching program and the role of the cooperating teacher in it. Prior to or early in the student teaching experience, expect your discussions and written communication with the college supervisor to center on the following topics:

- ☐ The basic rationale of the student teaching program such as the philosophy, principles, and objectives of the program as viewed from the perspective of the college.
- ☐ The college and state requirements including rules, guidelines, and requirements such as the minimum number of weeks, observation requirements, evaluation procedures, and a variety of reports.
- ☐ Information about the student teacher which outlines the student teacher's coursework and college activities, as well as necessary individual information about the student teacher.
- ☐ Basic concepts of supervision which define his role and outlines your responsibilities and strategies.
- ☐ Role of the teacher education institution in regard to support that can be expected from the college, what services will be provided, and where and how the college authority extends during student teaching in the public school.

It is beneficial for a college supervisor to be informed of the general nature of your school so that he is aware of the particular challenges and opportunities facing the student teacher. You can be helpful by informing the college supervisor of the following useful information:

- ☐ General profile of your class or classes that the student teacher will be teaching.
- ☐ Academic content and the time frame that the student teacher will teach.
- ☐ Established routines and procedures.

- [ ] Special projects or activities that will occur while the student teacher is there.
- [ ] General teaching styles and procedures used by the cooperating teacher.
- [ ] Available resource materials.
- [ ] Special events or vacation time scheduled by your school which occur during the student teaching experience.

ESTABLISHING RAPPORT

The cooperating teacher plus the college supervisor bring knowledge, insight, and perspective into the student teaching experience. You possess knowledge of the school and pupils as well as recent teaching experience. The college supervisor provides an increased understanding of the student teacher and a comprehensive view of the responsibilities and goals of teacher education in general and student teaching in particular. Both parties complement each other when they work together and share their skills and perspectives.

Slick (1998) notes that as the student teaching experience progresses, the cooperating teacher–college supervisor relationship evolves in positive and substantial ways. Common professional courtesies go a long way in helping develop rapport as you work closely with the college supervisor. Consider initiating these actions to build that professional relationship:

- [ ] Make a brief introductory contact prior to the start of the student teaching semester.
- [ ] Acknowledge the college supervisor's arrival to the classroom.
- [ ] Allow the student teacher to introduce the college supervisor to the students.
- [ ] Pre-plan time for observation and conferences with the student teacher and time for the cooperating teacher conference.
- [ ] Coordinate with others in the building that the supervisor may need to visit.
- [ ] Provide a map of the school or give a tour.
- [ ] Indicate restrooms and teacher's lounge.
- [ ] Identify any special protocol or routines at the school.
- [ ] Recommend parking areas.
- [ ] Explain check-in procedures for guests.

☐ Share contact information.

☐ Invite participation in lunch, school assemblies, and special events.

☐ Prepare updates, questions, and concerns about your student teacher's progress.

☐ Ready questions, concerns, gains, and ideas about your role.

Establishing rapport with the college supervisor extends beyond the cooperating teacher. Other individuals have an impact on your student teacher and those key members should also get to know the college supervisor. The introduction of the college supervisor to teachers, administration, support staff, aides, and volunteers falls to the hosting cooperating teacher. The mutual exchange of views and ideas from these contacts can be beneficial. Such communication also helps provide effective articulation between the higher education and cooperating school sectors.

PLANNED VISITS

Regular contacts with the college supervisor will probably occur every few weeks at the school site and possibly through additional phone conversations and Internet exchanges. This allows the college supervisor to be an active member of the triad.

Each college program has its own requirements for frequency of visits. The college supervisor notes more dramatic gains (or lack of progress) in between visits in contrast to the cooperating teacher who observes on a daily basis.

When visiting, the college supervisor will most likely want to observe the student teacher in an instructional setting and conduct a follow-up conference with the student teacher and then with you. Most often separate conferences will be held, but on occasion a conference with the triad will be conducted.

Value the time with the college supervisor. When conferring about the current analysis of and goals for your student teacher, the college supervisor can assist you by:

- Summarizing the student teacher's progress from a different perspective.
- Suggesting alternative procedures in methods, planning, conferences, and pupil contacts.
- Suggesting adjustments to the responsibility plan for your student teacher.
- Suggesting additional experiences for your student teacher.

- Suggesting supervisory techniques and strategies for the cooperating teacher.
- Reviewing requirements and ensuring that the college standards and state regulations are met.
- Setting additional time to counsel with student teachers who are having problems.
- Serving as a liaison between the student teacher and cooperating teacher.

Contacts with the college supervisor present you with an opportunity to secure other types of professional knowledge too. She provides information and assistance in such areas as:

- Developments in educational programs.
- Information concerning state standards, guidelines, and mandates.
- Knowledge about the broader educational scene and its implications for schools.
- Teaching skills.
- Resource materials.
- Employment opportunities.

Every effort should be made to accommodate and respect the time of each member of the triad. If scheduling a conference time during the day becomes too difficult, phone or online time after school hours becomes an option. Presetting time for the visiting day will allow the college supervisor to maximize the multiple dimensions of her role to the benefit of the others in the triad. It also sets the day's schedule for the equally busy cooperating teacher and student teacher.

INTERACTION WITH THE STUDENT TEACHER

You may wonder about the interaction between the college supervisor and student teacher. College supervisors render assistance to the student teacher in a number of ways when they visit your school. The most frequent types of exchanges are listed below:

- Gives supportive guidance from answering questions to counseling through a problem.
- Helps develop teaching skills by observations, conferences, resources, and ideas.
- Helps evaluate performance and set goals.
- Is a catalyst for professional reflection.
- Monitors progress on program and certification requirements.

- Serves as an intermediary in the event that there are disputes between you and your student teacher.

Caires and Almeida (2007) noted that the student teacher's perception of the college supervisor changed in positive ways as the student teaching experience progressed. Supervisors were noted for their structural and organizational attributes at the beginning but those decreased as interpersonal attributes became more valued at the end.

You help the working relationship of the triad by reinforcing the college supervisor's interpretations and monitoring progress with your student teacher between visits. You also add support by demonstrating confidence in the college supervisor and by noting her problem-solving skills.

The impact of the college supervisor depends, to a considerable extent, on the perceptions of the triad about the role she plays. The college supervisor makes contributions that would not otherwise be a dimension of the plan. She does this in a variety of ways in a great number of different situations. It is important for the cooperating teacher to nurture the relationship with the college supervisor since the pair works together to facilitate the growth of the student teacher.

Epilogue

Being a cooperating teacher is a rewarding yet complex role which you should undertake with confidence and clear direction. This is the first of the little instruction books that should have come with your student teacher to assist you in your supervisory role. It has guided you in defining the people and highlighting the foundation for the student teaching experience. Preparation is just the beginning of a successful student teaching experience.

What's next? Plenty! Is there more to the cooperating teacher role? Definitely! As the experience continues, more responsibilities are assumed by the student teacher so your analysis increases and your feedback becomes increasingly important. You will step back, yet strategically facilitate and encourage your student teacher to become independently responsible for all components of the teacher role. Before you know it, it will be time for the experience to wrap up and there will be an evaluation to complete and a letter of recommendation to write.

If you experience more of those what-do-I-do-now moments during the upcoming stages of your cooperating teacher role, we'll be here to help guide you through them. There are two more little instruction books planned so we sincerely hope that you'll journey with us through the rest of Student Teaching: The Cooperating Teacher Series:

Coaching a Student Teacher (Book 2)
Evaluating a Student Teacher (Book 3)

Ann and Marvin

What Would You Do? You can practice your supervisory skill using real-life situations. Access student teaching case studies at https://rowman.com/WebDocs/Bk1CaseStudies_online.pdf

---

References

Babkie, A. (1998). Twenty ways to work successfully with a student teacher. *Intervention in School and Clinic* 34(2): 115–17.

Barnes, S., and S. Edwards (1984). *Effective student teaching experience: A qualitative-quantitative study*. Retrieved from ERIC database (ED251441).

Caires, S., and L. S. Almeida (2007). Positive aspects of the teacher training supervision: The student teachers' perspective. *European Journal of Psychology of Education* 22(4): 515–28.

Costa, A. L., and R. J. Garmston (1987). Student teaching: Developing images of a profession. *Action in Teacher Education* 9(3): 5–11.

Cotton, E. G. (1981). A student teacher! What do I do now? *Kappa Delta Pi Record* 13(4): 100–1, 120.

Ganser, T., and M. A. Wham (1998). Voices of cooperating teachers: Professional contributions and personal satisfaction. *Teacher Education Quarterly* 25(2): 43–52.

Gibbs, L., and A. L. Montoya (1994). *The student teaching experience: Are student teachers the only ones to benefit?* Retrieved from ERIC database (ED373025).

Giebelhaus, C. R. (1995). *Revisiting a step-child: Supervision in teacher education*. Retrieved from ERIC database (ED391785).

Grossman, J. A., and D. L. Keller (1994). *A model for improving the pre-service teacher/ cooperating teacher diad*. Retrieved from ERIC database (ED377181).

Kagan, D. M. (1992). Professional growth among preservice and beginning teachers. *Review of Educational Research* 62(2): 129–69.

Looper, S. (1999). What your student teacher would like to tell you. *Teaching K–8* 30 (November–December): 58.

Moore, B. H. (1995). Inservicing through the back door: The impact of the student teacher upon the cooperating teacher. Paper presented at the Association of Teacher Educators, Detroit, MI.

Myers, I. B., and P. B. Myers (180). *Gifts differing*. Palo Alto, CA: Consulting Psychologists Press.

Seiferth, B. B., and M. Samuel (1984). Cooperating teachers: Why not the best? Retrieved from ERIC database (ED264176).

Sharpe, D. M. (1970). *A brief guide to secondary student teaching.* Terre Haute, IN: Indiana State University.

Shaw-Baker, M. H. (1995). Communication: The key to successful field experiences. In *Making the difference for teachers: The field experience in actual practice*, ed. G. A. Slick, 42–52. Thousand Oaks, CA: Corwin Press.

Slick, S. (1998). A university supervisor negotiates territory and status. *Journal of Teacher Education* 49(4): 306–15.

Trenfield, W. (1970). Your student teacher: An asset in the classroom? *Supervisors Quarterly* 6(2): 35–39.

Walker, D., and J. Archer (1999, October). Side by side: A true cooperative student teaching experience. Paper presented at the National Middle School Association Annual Conference, Orlando, FL.

Zimpher, N. L. (1980). A closer look at university student teacher supervision. *Journal of Teacher Education* 31(4): 11–15.

About the Authors

Marvin Henry served as professor of education and chairperson of curriculum and instruction at Indiana State University, where he was also a supervisor and field director for student teaching. He is a former president and a distinguished member of the Association of Teacher Educators as well as a recipient of its Outstanding Program in Teacher Education award.

Ann Weber served as instructional assistant professor in teacher education at Illinois State University. She collaborated with cooperating teachers while supervising hundreds of student teachers and was also the innovator in developing and teaching an online course in the supervision of student teachers.

The authors' experience, research, and passion in teacher education span over fifty-five years! They coauthored *Supervising Student Teachers the Professional Way*, 7th edition, which is a more extensive treatment of supervisory responsibilities, and its instructor's guide. They continue as speakers, writers, and advocates for the professional development of cooperating teachers. The authors can be reached at SSTTPW@gmail.com.